ANNAPOLIS POSTCARD COLLECTION

Portfolio Press

Kevin Fleming

Published by Portfolio Press, Ltd.
P.O. Box 626
Annapolis, Maryland 21404

For a free catalog or to reorder call:
1-800-233-3347

ISBN 0-929518-09-8

Printed in Hong Kong
89 90 91 92 93 5 4 3 2 1

What makes Annapolis special? Location alone makes Maryland's capital one of the loveliest cities in the United States. Overlooking the meeting of the Severn River and Chesapeake Bay, the city is a preeminent East Coast maritime center. Sailing yachts, power-boats, and historic Chesapeake Bay vessels all call this harbor home. Dazzling achievements in preservation help Annapolis retain a look and spirit befitting a city settled more than 300 years ago. The heart of the old city is protected as a Registered National Historic Landmark; Royal Governor Sir Francis Nicholson could still find his way around town by following the street plan he designed in 1696. Georgian mansions from the city's golden era recall the economic and political fortunes of men who shaped the history of Annapolis and the newly formed nation.

The lively presence of midshipmen from the United States Naval Academy and students from unconventional St. John's College keeps Annapolis in step with the times.

This small-town city of 34,000 mingles yacht owners with oyster shuckers, weekend sailors with Bay-bred watermen, and families who have lived here for generations with newcomers chasing the waterfront-property dream.

From political pomp to Naval Academy drills to the sail-filled Chesapeake to quiet moments with neighbors, award-winning photographer Kevin Fleming captures the myriad faces of Annapolis. This postcard collection contains many of his favorite photographs from his bestselling book *ANNAPOLIS* published by Portfolio Press.

Glad to come home to Annapolis, Kevin Fleming covers the world as a photographer for *National Geographic*. Assignments since 1979 have taken him into war and famine in Somalia, to the Mediterranean for a re-creation of the voyage of Ulysses on a replica of a late Bronze Age galley, and put him on a dogsled in northern Canada for an in-depth portrait of the Hudson's Bay Company. He has turned his camera on Florida, Maine, New Zealand, and the almost mystical world of high-energy physics. While reporting on the Sinai Peninsula in 1981, he came under the assassins' gunfire that killed Egyptian President Anwar Sadat. Unharmed, he escaped with some of the few photographs of that tragic moment.

Annapolis, Maryland

Thousands of people pick their way through hundreds of crabs at the Annapolis Rotary Club Crab Feast held annually at the Navy-Marine Corps Memorial Stadium.

From *ANNAPOLIS* Copyright © 1988 by Kevin Fleming Portfolio Press, P.O. Box 626, Annapolis, MD 21404

Annapolis, Maryland

Pricey real estate today, Cornhill Street was modestly developed by middle-class merchants and craftsmen during the 18th and 19th centuries.

From *ANNAPOLIS* Copyright © 1988 by Kevin Fleming Portfolio Press, P.O. Box 626, Annapolis, MD 21404

Annapolis, Maryland

Fledgling ospreys, or fish hawks, prepare to leave their
nest atop a Severn River navigation marker.

Annapolis, Maryland

*Floating docks extend the City Dock for the annual
October boat shows.*

Annapolis, Maryland

A high-rise garage for powerboats on the South River
helps solve the perennial problem of docking space.

From *ANNAPOLIS* Copyright © 1988 by Kevin Fleming Portfolio Press, P.O. Box 626, Annapolis, MD 21404

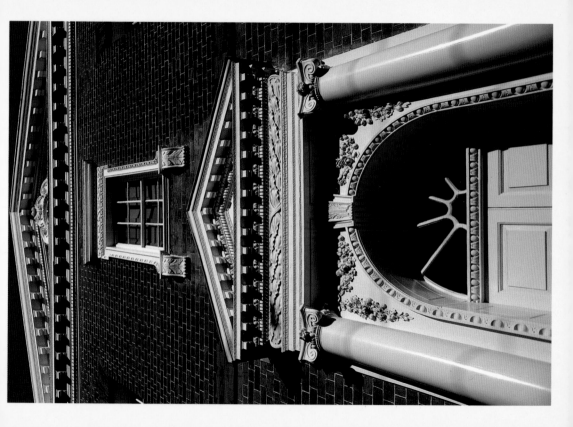

Annapolis, Maryland

Testimony to colonial wealth, the Palladian door of the Hammond-Harwood House has been acclaimed as one of the loveliest in all of America.

Annapolis, Maryland

Gracefully marking the entrance to the South River since 1875, the Thomas Point Light was the last manned lighthouse on the Chesapeake before the Coast Guard automated it in 1986.

Annapolis, Maryland

Autumn comes to the Edward Dorsey house on Prince George Street, built in the mid 1700's.

From *ANNAPOLIS* Copyright © 1988 by Kevin Fleming Portfolio Press, P.O. Box 626, Annapolis, MD 21404

Annapolis, Maryland

Main Street rises toward St. Anne's Episcopal Church.

From *ANNAPOLIS* Copyright © 1988 by Kevin Fleming Portfolio Press, P.O. Box 626, Annapolis, MD 21404

Annapolis, Maryland

Where the Chesapeake is at its narrowest, the William Preston Lane, Jr., Memorial Bridge links Anne Arundel County with Kent Island on Maryland's Eastern Shore.

Annapolis, Maryland

*The world's largest college dormitory, Bancroft Hall houses
4,500 students of the United States Naval Academy.*

Annapolis, Maryland

A sea of plebes gather for a swearing-in ceremony, the beginning of four years of academic and military discipline designed to train officers for the Navy or Marine Corps.

Annapolis, Maryland

Heat topples a midshipman during a dress parade competition among the 36 companies of the Brigade of Midshipmen.

From *ANNAPOLIS* Copyright © 1988 by Kevin Fleming Portfolio Press, P.O. Box 626, Annapolis, MD 21404

Annapolis, Maryland

Early morning waterskiers leave their signatures on the South River.

Annapolis, Maryland

*Floating docks extend the City Dock for the annual
October boat shows.*

Annapolis, Maryland

Streets radiate from St. Anne's and the Maryland State House toward the Severn River and Chesapeake Bay.

Annapolis, Maryland

*A patriotic streak has always run through Annapolis,
the capital of the United States for nine months in
1783 and 1784.*

Annapolis, Maryland

*The "painted ladies" of Annapolis, early 20th-century
frame houses grace Conduit, Market and Revel Streets
near Spa Creek.*

Annapolis, Maryland

The promise of autumn calls a sloop down Whitehall Creek as dawn breaks over the Chesapeake Bay.

From *ANNAPOLIS* Copyright © 1988 by Kevin Fleming Portfolio Press, P.O. Box 626, Annapolis, MD 21404

Annapolis, Maryland

Streets radiate from the city's highest elevation, reserved for the Maryland State House, the oldest State Capitol in continuous use.

From *ANNAPOLIS* Copyright © 1988 by Kevin Fleming Portfolio Press, P.O. Box 626, Annapolis, MD 21404

Annapolis, Maryland

_"Ego alley," the channel into City Dock, becomes a
congested promenade as boats of every description
jockey to see and be seen._

Annapolis, Maryland

Hibernating in dry dock, boats will be cleaned and repainted for the spring season.

Annapolis, Maryland

A beacon to mariners for centuries, the Maryland State House rises over Annapolis harbor.

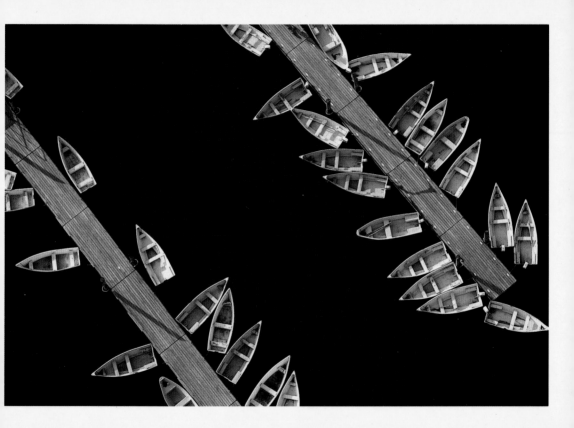

Annapolis, Maryland

*Like leaves on a tree branch, rowboats move with the
wind at Sandy Point State Park.*

Annapolis, Maryland

*Saved from demolition and adapted for 20th-century living,
the buildings in the one-third-square-mile Historic District
represent 17 architectural styles from 1675 to 1930.*

Annapolis, Maryland

A sunset view of the harbor embraces symbols of the city: the spire of St. Anne's Episcopal Church, the capitol dome, and the Naval Academy's Halsey Field House.

Annapolis, Maryland

*In the glow of a summer Chesapeake evening, sailboats
fly wind-catching spinnakers in the Wednesday-night
races sponsored by the Annapolis Yacht Club.*

Annapolis, Maryland

William Paca, a signer of the Declaration of Independence,
completed his 37-room Georgian mansion and two-acre
garden in 1765.

From *ANNAPOLIS* Copyright © 1988 by Kevin Fleming Portfolio Press, P.O. Box 626, Annapolis, MD 21404

Annapolis, Maryland

As the Sun rises, a trotline crabber heads up Whitehall Creek.

Annapolis, Maryland

An Annapolis tradition, The Eastport Yacht Club's
Christmas Lights Parade is a favorite holiday event.